MW00637733

The Last Harvest
Truck Farmers in the Deep South

BY PERRY DILBECK

WITH A CONCLUSION BY TOM RANKIN

THE CENTER FOR AMERICAN PLACES

SANTA FE AND STAUNTON

CENTER BOOKS ON THE AMERICAN SOUTH

GEORGE F. THOMPSON, SERIES FOUNDER AND DIRECTOR

Contents

Introduction

DURING A RECENT VISIT TO MY HOMETOWN of McDonough, Georgia (2000 pop. 8,493), I noticed an alarming trend. Much of the farmland around my home had rapidly disappeared due to a sharp growth in population not only in my immediate neighborhood, but also in the surrounding areas and for many miles away. Replacing the fertile landscape, numerous subdivisions have been constructed in order to accommodate this swirl of people migrating into the area about twenty-five miles southeast of Atlanta. Twenty years ago, there were only sixteen houses on my rural road of three miles, but today more than 2,000 houses exist. Likewise, the large-scale commercial farming industry has nearly destroyed the business of many small independent farmers here and has forced them to make money the only way they can—by selling their farmland.

America's small farms have been disappearing for decades. The number of farms in the nation has fallen from nearly seven million in 1935 to about two million today, with the total amount of land under cultivation remaining around one billion acres. The average size of a farm has increased from about 100 acres to nearly 500 acres—a fact which obviously points to the elimination of many small farms. The main force behind this shift to bigger farms is the economies of scale. The technology and equipment available to modern farmers can be used most efficiently and profitably in large-scale operations. As a result, most small-scale farmers find themselves seeking jobs on the side just to make ends meet. Reluctantly, older farmers are no longer training their sons and daughters in this declining profession.

I can still remember an old farmer we called "Butterbean" who lived just up the street from my family. He had several hundred acres of farmland, and he would regularly stand along the roadside waving to anyone who might happen to drive by throughout the day. It seems as though it was just yesterday when my friends and I spent many summer hours playing army and hunting in Butterbean's fields. Now, a large-scale subdivision is being erected on what was once Butterbean's property.

In an effort to safeguard the lifestyle of Butterbean and other small-scale Georgia farmers, I felt compelled to create a tribute to the surviving workers of the land by recording their lifestyles with the camera and their stories as well. In documenting these individuals, I mainly concentrate on older farmers whose lands and homesteads have been passed down through many generations, who started farming as kids before the Depression when there were only mules to drive the plow. Within this group, I focus my attention on "truck farmers," those who typically own fewer than forty acres of land and who grow food for their family. Survival is dependent upon selling any surplus at local farmer's markets, along the roadside from the back of a truck, or at a simple stand in the front yard.

Unlike other photographers who often portray the hurt and despair of farmers, I strive to display the wonderful pride and dignity these farmers exude in their daily lives. I look for a face that shows the signs of a vigorous life, and I usually document the oldest of the farming generations whose faces and demeanor are so appealing. My photographs provide glimpses into the lifestyles of these very noble people. I attempt to capture the subtle and often hidden moments in order to allow viewers to see beyond the surface of reality. Since 1996, I have photographed and interviewed dozens of small-scale farming families in Alabama, Florida, Georgia, and Tennessee, but for this book present only those in my home place—the counties surrounding Atlanta.

To find interesting subjects, I usually just get in the car and drive for miles and miles and look. One afternoon, I passed a farmer sitting at a quaint little vegetable stand alongside a small country road. This particular farmer turned out to be one of my favorite subjects, Jack Parris. Locally known for his wonderful peas, tomatoes, and corn, Jack was more than happy to help me in my endeavors. He is a very trusting character who often leaves his produce on a stand and allows neighbors and strangers alike to put money in a milk bucket in return for the produce they take home. I have watched Jack work for hours shelling peas by hand only to charge his customers a few dollars. His enjoyment is not in the little money he makes, but in the smiles he puts on his customers faces when they tell him how sweet a cantaloupe was at Sunday dinner or how delicious their tomato sandwich was for lunch.

Horace Parker, a ninety-year-old farmer from Covington, Georgia (pop. 11,547), recalls the days when the road in front of his farm was a single-lane dirt road with very little traffic. "I remember when the only vehicles you would see on the road were a mailman or school bus, and the only reason I ever had to go to town was if a bolt broke on my tractor. You were lucky if you saw ten cars go by in a single day," said Parker. He reflects back to these glorious years of steady farming and remembers Daisy, his recently deceased wife of forty-eight years. Tears slowly appeared in Parker's eyes as he told the sad story of how Daisy died in their kitchen one autumn morning, the victim of an unknown brain tumor. Parker is left with three children, seven grandchildren, and three brothers and sisters who come to visit him every month.

Several of my photographs depict J. W. Clark picking corn in the field during his annual harvest celebration. Neighbors and other friends gather for this event to share stories and help shuck, cut, and can the fresh corn. This past year was especially important to Clark because he had overcome a serious health problem earlier in the year, and he did not know if he would even be able to plant. When asked about the continuing decline of farmland, he replied, "Yep, I remember when there were thirty-three dairy farms in Henry County alone. Now there is only one. Subdivisions are squeezing us farmers out. You just can't get no land to farm on in this county. One has to go to South Georgia for that, and I'm too old to do that."

While photographing Clark, I came across his wonderful companion Patti, a hound dog that follows Clark wherever he goes. In the background, Patti is barking and Clark declares, "Patti, c'mon. Let's go to the store." Patti barks and slowly makes her way to the truck. She rides in the truck every morning to go to Rolands, the local general store. "She loves to ride," Clark says. "I leave the door open lot of time if I think it's gonna storm when she can get in." With a little luck, Clark and Patti will be around for next year's harvest.

Charlie Thomas, Sr., now eighty-six years old, has lived in White County, Georgia (pop. 19,944), his entire life and has been farming since he was just a young lad. Thomas has much experience growing various crops such as cotton, sorghum, cane, corn, beans,

Page to be corrected in final version.

PAVING TO SUBURBAN, 2002

potatoes, and tomatoes. His specialty is an old-time cornfield bean, the seed for which he has been able to trace back to more than 125 years. Thomas says that farming is what keeps him going in life, and he expects to keep it up until he dies.

Leavell Smith was born in Vienna, Georgia (pop. 2,973), and his family moved to Newnan, Georgia (pop. 16,242), when he was seven years old. Now at age seventy-six, Smith still lives in Newnan and has been farming for about sixty years on his own. A former trapper, Smith grows a variety of crops, including okra, purple hull peas, corn, and collards. He also grows several varieties of watermelons, including a black diamond, midnight, jubilee, and Dixie Lee.

All of these farmers live passionate lives and work hard in small places. Although their precious farmland is quickly vanishing, each farmer is filled with the joy, enthusiasm, and assurance of a job well done. The memories of their wonderfully satisfying lives will continue to sustain each farmer until they pass away. Perhaps all of the technological advances and the rapidly growing population in the Southeast are merely signs of the times, better times according to some. I often wonder, however, if this new generation of farmers, who adhere to the new demands of advanced farming, will ever truly possess all of the down-home ingredients that make the small-scale truck farmers in this book such genuine and unique people.

The Last Harvest

Jack Parris

I had two mules, my brother had two mules, and, with a turning plow, we plowed all this farm and that one, too. We made twenty-five bales of cotton that year and 'bout 300 bushels of corn, and I made a wagon load of sweet potatoes. And we had three big fattenin' hogs apiece and two milk cows apiece. And we's livin' like high on the hog then. But we didn't have no money. We's still broke.

JACK PARRIS, 2001

SPRING PLOWING, 2003

JACK'S FARM, 2003

SHELLING PEAS, 2002

FAMILY SCALE, 2001

I put a set of scales out there on a little ole table I got, and I put a bucket on a little ole tree there. And I put stuff out there, and folks comes along and weighs it and gets it and drops money in that little ole bucket. A lady asks me the other day says, "Don't you get beat outta nothing'?" I said, "Well, I don't know. I don't weigh what I put out here, and I don't know what I got. So, what you don't know don't hurt you." She laughed at me and said, "I guess you're right." I don't think anybody beat me. I trust everybody. If he needs it and he's hungry, let 'em take it on. If he's got the money to pay fer it, I spect 'em to pay fer it. I done good. Last year, I sold 'bout 1,800 pounds of maters on that little ole table.

JACK'S STAND, 2002

JACK AND LATE WIFE AGNES, 2001

When I moved out here, there wasn't even a phone,
wasn't even a power line through here. I moved here
in '43 on this little bitty pig trail. There weren't no
houses around, but now you can't get outta the house
without steppin' on somebody else's yard. Now, it's just
bumper to bumper. They got a four-way stop sign now,
and all the roads are paved. And sometimes cars are
lined up half a mile down there just tryin' to get through
this stop sign. So I don't know what the country's comin' to.

Horace Parker

*I started out in the garden with Mother settin' out
onions in the Spring of the year. She taught me how
to hoe 'em and tend to 'em. And Daddy put me
to plowin' when I was ten years old.*

HORACE PARKER, 1998

13

PICKING COLLARDS, 1998

A LIFE'S WORK, 1998

PARKER'S BARN, 1998

16

BARNYARD CAT, 1998

A fellow asked me, "How come everything else is burning up and those butter beans is green?" I told him, "When I planted them, I asked God to bless them. And He just turned them green. And they been growing green ever since."

A CERTAIN PONDERING, 1998

COLLECTING RAIN, 2001

MARTIN'S NEST, 2001

*When I first got here, 'bout the only traffic there
was the school bus and the mailman. Wasn't but
a very few cars passing during the day. Now,
you can go out there and count ten cars in
a short few minutes. Sometimes you can have
to wait for fifteen cars to pass before you can find
a slot to get out.*

PARKER'S PREP, 1998

1949 FORD 8N TRACTOR, 2001

OLD FREEZER AND WOODEN CHAIR, 1998

Leavell Smith

I been farming 'bout sixty years on my own.
I was born in Vienna, Georgia, and come here
[to Newman] when I was seven years old
and stayed here the rest of my life.

GATHERING WATERMELONS, 2003

It's hard work and, when the older people die, the young folks won't do this. There's more money in working and doing other business than there is in farming. And you don't have as many liabilities. You know what you're gonna get. In farming, you have to take what you can get. There's a lot of risk. For the last few years, I ain't even broke even. I ain't broke even at all. [I continue to do it because] it's just somethin' that's in my blood, I reckon.

LEAVELL SMITH, 2003

WATERMELON PATCH #1, 2003

SMITH HARVESTING WATERMELONS, 2003

FRUIT AND VEGETABLE STAND, 2003

BUTTERBEANS #2, 2003

33

Well, I'm just going one year at a time. I don't even know if I'll be able next year. If I hadn't gotten better this summer, I wouldn't have been able to do it. It's comin' to a close. I know that. I don't know when, but it ain't too much longer that I can stand it. It's a lot of hard, dirty work. That's what it is. [But, I enjoy it because] I like to see things grow. I like to see things grow.

SMITH AT SATURDAY MARKET, 2003

Emerson "Red" Berry

I used to pick cotton long time ago. Now, people come from miles around to buy Red's melons. I had the best 'round these parts.

RED BERRY #5, 2003

RED BERRY AND HIS 1957 FARMALL TRACTOR, 2001

When I wasn't working in the fields, I would always tinker with Farmall tractors of all sorts. Not many people know how to fix these, so everyone will bring them to me.

Thomas Singley

We been living on the farm since 1891. My granddaddy
died in 1911, and my grandmother died in 1944. My mother
bought the farm from her brothers and sisters in 1945
for $3,200, which included 100 acres and a little shack
on the hill. My oldest brother got killed in the war, so
my mother had his insurance money to buy the farm with.
We took the farm then, and we been in this house ever since.
I now have about fifty acres and give the rest to my son, Mike.

THOMAS SINGLEY WITH A BABY GOAT, 2003

SINGLEY'S PLACE, 2003

Well, I grow mostly sweet corn. I just came up with a new one called Avalon. It's a triple sweet corn. Boy, everybody loves it. It's really good out of the freezer, too, just like fresh corn ya just picked off the stalk. My grandkids, every time they come by, they just ask Granny, "You cooked any corn today?" Also I grow Homestead tomatoes with a strong taste to them. I have customers come as far as Athens and Blairsville to buy them. They can't find any homegrown ones with a lot of acid in them, so they come way down here to buy them from me.

CORN DELIVERY, 2003

SINGLEY'S STAND, 2003

GRANDKIDS JOSH AND MICHAEL SINGLEY, 2003

"Ready to sell?" I said, "I done told you. You come talk to my wife when I die—not before. You can make your offer when I die, because she has four or five others waitin' to make offers." Every week I get a call. "I looked in the Henry County tax book and saw you have 47.2 acres. What would you take it for?" "It ain't for sale." That don't keep them from calling.

Lawson Chafin

I just turned eighty years old and was born and raised in Henry County. We started out with two mules and we got another when I was twelve years old. In '52, I bought my first set of planters and cultivators for an Allis Chalmers tractor. We used to have a black man that lived on our place and that helped us farm named Henry. He taught me as much about farming as anybody I've ever been around.

LAWSON CHAFIN, 1997

LAWSON'S HAYFIELD AT DUSK, 1998

In the early days, we went to the gin mill and country store.
Now, none of that is left except for Miller's store. Miller's
is the only store you can go and sit down. It used to be
the only mill around here. Going to the mill was a big event . . .
If the weather was pretty, you would stay in the field for
three weeks, but when it rained you knew you were going
to the mill the next morning to get cornmeal ground for feed
for the cornery and wheats for 'shorts' for the hogs. Everybody
had three or four big hogs that they killed every year. Back then,
nearly every country store had a book that thick with accounts
from the farmers. He feed 'em, a lot of them farmers and his help,
until the fall when the final crops came in.

Euston Slaton

I am ninety-seven years old and lived in Franklin County
most of my life. Farming has been in my family for eight
generations. We cultivated and saved wheat, corn, and
cotton with two mules, over sixty acres that was won, in
the early 1800s Georgia Land Lottery, by my great-grandaddy.

EUSTON SLATON IN HIS OLD TOBACCO BARN, 1997

DAY'S END, SLATON COMING HOME, 1999

When Roosevelt was President back in 1933, cotton was
one cent a pound, and the government would send a man
out to tell us how much cotton we could plant that season.
In 1949, I was able to get a real Massy Harris tractor.
It took me four years to pay for it.

J. W. Clark

*My Daddy died when I was eight years old, and, well,
I helped [on the farm]. When I got a little bigger, I went
to plowin'. We had a tenant that would work our crop,
and we'd hoe it and kept it clean. And then we'd pick
cotton and gather our own crop, and then we'd gather
some for other folks. We had it pretty rough.*

CORN HARVEST, 1997

WINDMILL, 1998

CLARK'S PLACE, 1998

Every mornin', when I go to the store, she'll get in
the truck, ready to go. She sits over on the fer side,
and she'll go down to the store and sit out as long
as I stay. And then we'll come back, and she'll get out
and ramble around. She loves to ride. I leave the door
open lot of time if I think it's gonna storm when she
can get in.

PATTI BESIDE J. W.'S 1980 CHEVY TRUCK, 1998

CUTTING CORN, 1997

CORN STALK, 1997

GEORGIA PECANS, 1998

64

I planted those trees, and it took a good seven to eight years before they even startin' bearing. I gathered the pecans when the crows and squirrels didn't try to get 'em. I killed a crow just about every year and hung 'em up out there. It would keep 'em out some, but they would still slip in there when I was gone.

Charlie Thomas Senior

*In the 1920s, you know, there was very few automobiles
in White County. And, of course, the farmin' was all done
by horse and mule, and now it's done by tractor. Yeah,
my Daddy, he used to keep some good mules, and
I'd wear 'em out for him.*

CHARLIE THOMAS SENIOR, 2003

THE CHARLIE THOMAS SENIOR HOME, 2003

68

CHARLIE'S OLD-TIME CORNFIELD BEANS, 2003

CORNFIELD BEANS #2, 2003

70

HOMEGROWN BIRD FEEDER, 2003

GOURDS, 1998

Well, I probably will cut back a good bit [next year].
I ain't gonna completely quit, 'cause that's what keeps
me a goin'.

Buster Brown

Returning after WWI, my father bought this piece of land in 1932 with $500 that the government gave him. I was six years old when we moved here.

BUSTER WITH CAT, 2002

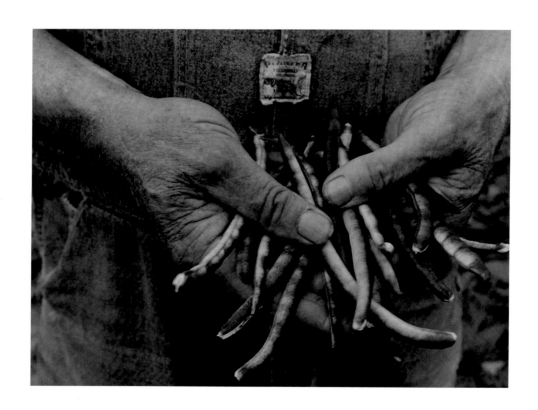

BUSTER'S PURPLE HULL PEAS, 2002

Now, I'm seventy-five years old and I grow okra, Pink-eye purple peas, Yellow-merit corn, and squash for me and my family. The rest I give away to friends and family. It's been kinda tough the last couple of years trying to keep deer from eatin' everything up.

Alton Alexander

I was born and raised in Henry County in 1937
and specialized in growing soybeans and wheat.
Now, I just sell a tiny bit of Mississippi sidewinder
peas, cantaloupe, and corn to help ends meet.
The government took everything I owned [for a highway]
and left me with a few acres of land. I had to sell the rest
and most of my equipment.

ALTON ALEXANDER, 2003

FRANK HEMPHILL AND ABE, 2003

HEMPHILL'S CORNFIELD TRACTOR, A 1954 FORD 600 WORKMASTER, 2003

PAUL HARRIS, EARLY IN THE SEASON, 1997

PAUL HARRIS ON THE BUSHHOG, 1997

Afterword

*Farmin's the only thing that you can go broke every year
and come back the next year and do the same thing.
You go to the bank, and they loan you the money to farm
with. You can always borrow money to farm. They take all
you made, and you'd have to do the same thing next year.*

−Jack Parris

JACK PARRIS AND CUSTOMER, 2003

Conclusion: Careful Tending
by Tom Rankin

The grower of trees, the gardener, the man born to farming,
whose hands reach into the ground and sprout,
to him the soil is a divine drug. He enters into death
yearly, and comes back rejoicing.
— Wendell Berry, from "The Man Born to Farming"

THE SOUTHERN TRUCK FARMER—the small produce
gardener who grows a crop annually on modest plots of well-tended land in an age of
endlessly expanding fields in a dominant American agriculture—is a symbol of what's left
of a human scale in a world gone big. Little is more revealing, or more fundamentally
hopeful, than a person laying out straight rows of vegetables and carefully bringing them
along through weed and bug infestations, too much or too little rain, helping them emerge
from native soil inch by inch until the days of ripening. To these farmers, says the poet
Wendell Berry, himself a small-scale farmer, "the soil is a divine drug."[1]

I learned something about growing a vegetable garden as a young child in
Kentucky, watching my grandmother plant and weed and pick in her yard, and then later

through a deep apprenticeship in my own garden behind my house. A man who worked for both my grandparents and my parents carefully introduced me to the correct way to use a spade and hoe, to the laying out of rows and the forming of hills for tomatoes and squash, to how to keep a garden 'clean' of weeds and other harmful invasions. From the age of nine or ten, we would signal spring with the ritual of planting, believing as much in the act of doing it as in the possibilities of harvest. The men whom Perry Dilbeck photographed are human testimonies to this timeless tradition where hard manual work meets a gentle tending to the land, as truck farmers repeat their optimistic start each year. To be sure, these men farm for a livelihood, but it is a way of living they have chosen, and through their choice they have remained in touch with the ground.

Southern truck farming began as a possible alternative to the perpetual dependence on cotton and other cash crops throughout the American South. The reliance on cotton, in particular, left many small farmers exposed and vulnerable to the ebb and flow of market prices and the success of harvest. Sometime after the Civil War, with transportation options expanding, truck farming began to mature throughout the region. By 1900, argues historian James L. McCorkle, Jr., the increased demand for fresh vegetables and fruits provided new opportunities for small Southern farmers. With the building of more railroads and greater options to transport produce by water, the South experienced a rise in truck farming. As McCorkle explains, "King Cotton found himself sharing his domain with, among others, King Strawberry, King Spud, King Lettuce, King Cabbage, and King Celery." Truck farming was, in the words of one Texas farmer, "more profitable and more pleasant than cotton and corn."[2]

Today, truck farming is popularly thought to refer to the Dodges, Toyotas, Nissans, Chevys, and Fords that are used to transport produce from field to market on the beds of trucks that serve as display surfaces for a well-grown crop. The term "truck," however, has much older origins: the *Oxford English Dictionary* defines the verb "to truck" as "to exchange for profit; to barter"; an 1866 description said, "A truck garden, a truck farm, is a market-garden or farm"; and a nineteenth-century definition of "trucker" reads, "one who grows 'truck' or garden produce for market, a truck-gardener or truck-farmer."[3] Whatever we know the 'truck' modifier to refer to, we do understand the truck farmer to be a small grower of vegetables and fruits who has a hand in both growing and moving the produce to a local market. He's often assisted by family members or co-workers. Among his many skills are an ability to plant and harvest his crop, fix and modify machinery, advertise and sell what he grows, and pass along his knowledge and skills to others in his family and community.

Perry Dilbeck's truck farmers are certainly more attuned to the weather, the ground, and the hopeful harvest than they are to the origins and multiple meanings of the term 'truck'. Nevertheless, they are part of a long lineage of careful, watchful farm workers who transform small pieces of ground year by year into food and a way of life. Endlessly positive in their commitment to the land—they could never survive without a deep well of hopeful confidence—their annual planting triggers a new resurrection that comes, first, with the initial germination and the revealing of new plants and, then, with the next harvest.

Dilbeck is no newcomer or stranger to these men or their kind. Growing up in Henry County, outside Atlanta, he has observed farmers such as his childhood neighbor

SUNFLOWERS, 2003

known simply as Butterbean. Dilbeck cherishes the rural scenes and environments that farmers such as Butterbean inherited, create, and manage. His photographs show us the way these farmers mark the land, how their aesthetic becomes part of our Southern rural landscapes. Dilbeck has also witnessed the gradual demise of many farms as fields have turned into domestic subdivisions, and he praises these men and grieves the passing of their ways through his artistry and field work.

Dilbeck's images—made with a Holga, the simplest of plastic cameras—are reverential even in their darkest corners, and his entire body of work—pictures and words—is a liturgical offering to the cultural and visual richness of these men and their care of land and community. His photographs document these farmers and their agricultural spaces, but they do much more than simply record: they are at once an honest reflection of well-lived lives and transformative expressions of Dilbeck's respectful and creative vision.

Like the farmers he pictures who have plowed and planted and fertilized and harvested, Dilbeck has also carefully tended to his own garden, a diminishing field of hard working and independent truck farmers whom he has rendered with the same care they give their freshest produce. These men aren't the "last" as in the "final" farmers, but they represent a way of being on the land that is quickly passing. These men learned to plow behind a mule and now find themselves at the end of a long row of years where farming has changed along with the rest of their community. They've chosen to stay close: close to home, close to the land, close to the cycles of season and life, even as to farm a postage-stamp size garden of native soil year after year is less and less common. And the knowledge that comes from that act of tending to what's close at hand year after year is becoming harder for us to locate. While other younger farmers—the organic growers and farm-to-market entrepreneurs, among them—are committed to the local growing of fresh produce, they don't have the historical memory of these men. Unlike these men, they can't identify from experience all that's present in the rearview mirror.

GRINDSTONE AND BIRDBATH, 1999

91

I knew a woman, the daughter of a Mississippi Delta farmer, who recalled that locals said of her father that he "covered all the ground he stood on." A profound statement not meant literally, she told me this out of deep respect for her long-passed father. He was, to her and others who spoke of him, a man of integrity, solid and stable. He was grounded and dependable. And, for her, nothing could be more a compliment than to describe someone as "covering the ground he stood on."[4] These men, likewise, cover their ground. And Dilbeck, by taking us there and revealing to us these lives and places, makes visible an all-important piece of our cultural ground, lives of wisdom and work and productivity becoming more obscured by our suburbanized landscapes and more mechanized lives that are addicted to commuting.

Farmer Jack Parris tells how he sells his tomatoes through an honor system. He leaves his produce and scales on a table, trusting that his customers will weigh what they want and leave their money for what they take home. Clearly, Parris is an old-fashioned believer in the best of human nature, undaunted by a lady who assumes he would get "beat outta" his profit. "I trust everybody," he tells Dilbeck. "If he needs it and he's hungry, let 'em take it on. If he's got the money to pay fer it, I spect 'em to pay fer it." Parris believes that, whatever has happened in the past—whether his customers paid him fairly or took advantage of his trust—he has done well, selling plenty of tomatoes that make him more than satisfied. Believing that people will do him right propels him, it seems. And it's belief that Horace Parker holds out when asked how he keeps his butter beans so green. "When I planted them," he tells the fellow, "I asked God to bless them. And He just turned them green. And they been growing green ever since."

Whatever belief these truck farmers have, they share it generously with their customers and are models of a well-lived traditional life. They offer the best fruits and vegetables while also sharing personal perspectives drawn from a life of cultivation, seeds of wisdom and experience that only get passed along from one person and one generation to another, at roadside stands and by those born to farming. Their sharing, thankfully, is a gift they extended to Dilbeck and, through him, carefully and eloquently to us.

Wendell Berry's "The Seeds," a poem that evokes the power of planting and place, speaks to the life and acts of the small-scale farmer—and also to the wise choice that Perry Dilbeck made by photographing close "to his own place," sowing for us his compelling images and stories:

> . . . But the sower
> going forth to sow sets foot
> into time to come, the seeds falling
> on his own place. He has prepared a way
> for his life to come to him, if it will.
> Like a tree, he has given roots
> To the earth, and stands free.[5]

NOTES

1. Wendell Berry, "The Man Born to Farming," *Collected Poems, 1957-1982* (San Francisco: North Point Press, 1985).

2. James L. McCorkle, Jr., "Moving Perishables to Market: Southern Railroads and the Nineteenth Century Origins of Truck Farming," in *Agricultural History*, Volume 6, No. 1, Winter 1992.

3. *Oxford English Dictionary Online*, Oxford University Press, 2006.

4. Personal conversation with Emma Knowlton Lytle, of Perthshire, Mississippi.

5. Wendell Berry, "The Seeds," in *Collected Poems, 1957–1982* (San Francisco: North Point Press, 1985).

Acknowledgments

This book is dedicated to my wife Deborah, and to Ed and Lois Dilbeck, the best parents anyone could ask for.

Special thanks to George F. Thompson and Amber K. Lautigar, of the Center for American Places, and to the University of Georgia Press, the Blue Earth Alliance, David Skolkin, Tom Rankin, John McLeod, Debbie Fleming Caffery, Roy Flukinger, Tommy Irvin, Brooks Jensen, and Bill Wylie.

I am most grateful to the farmers who shared their lives with me: Alton Alexander, Emerson "Red" Berry, Buster Brown, Lawson Chafin, J. W. Clark, Paul Harris, Frank Hemphill, Horace Parker, Jack Parris, Thomas Singley, Euston Slaton, Leavell Smith, and Charlie Thomas Senior.

MY BUDDY, 2002

I also appreciate greatly the support from the following people and institutions:
Malcolm Edwards, Natalie Fobes, Alejandro Tomas, Texas Photographic Society, D. Clark Evans, Paula Wallace at the Savannah College of Art and Design, The Art Institute of Atlanta, Martye Jeffords, Richard Newman, Joe and Sue Dishman, Fred Dilbeck, Steve Anchell, Alisa McWhinnie, Eric Gringnol, Photomedia Center, Henry Rasmussen, Jean Caslin, the Houston Center for Photography, Kari Croop, Jim Jordan, Pat Fleishacker, John Knuth, Clare Glassell, Paul Clarvi, Craig Stevens, Michelle Bates, Katheryn Demicco, Kirsten Rian, Blue Sky Gallery, Steve Goff, the Callanwolde Fine Arts Center in Alanta, Laurie Allan, Roger Maile, David Bigwood, Robert Graham, Sy Safransky, Milton Lowery, Joel Conison, and Trudy Wischemann.

About the Author and the Essayist

Perry Dilbeck (b. 1965, Atlanta, Georgia) has been a full-time instructor of photography at the Art Institute of Atlanta since 1998. His photographs have appeared in *Black & White, The British Journal of Photography, LensWork, Photo Art International, Photo District News*, and numerous other magazines. Dilbeck's photographs are in the permanent collections of the Museum of Fine Arts in Houston, the Harry Ransom Humanities Research Center at the University of Texas at Austin, Photo-Eye Books & Prints in Santa Fe, and the Savannah College of Art and Design, among others. He has had dozens of group and one-person exhibitions in galleries throughout the United States.

Tom Rankin is Associate Professor of the Practice of Art and Director of the Center for Documentary Studies at Duke University. His books include *Sacred Space: Photographs from the Mississippi Delta* (1993), which received the Mississippi Institute of Arts and Letters Award for Photography, *Deaf Maggie Lee Sayre: Photographs of a River Life* (1995), *Faulkner's World: The Photographs of Martin J. Dain* (1997), and *Local Heroes Changing America* (2000).

The Center for American Places is a tax-exempt 501(c)(3) nonprofit organization, founded in 1990, whose educational mission is to enhance the public's understanding of, appreciation for, and affection for the natural and built environment. Underpinning this mission is the belief that books provide an indispensable foundation for comprehending and caring for the places where we live, work, and explore. Books endure. Books make a difference. Books are gifts to civilization.

With offices in Santa Fe, New Mexico, and Staunton, Virginia, Center editors bring to publication as many as thirty books per year under the Center's own imprint or in association with publishing partners. Center books have won or shared more than ninety editorial awards and citations, including multiple best-books honors in more than thirty academic fields.

The Center is also engaged in other outreach programs that emphasize the interpretation of place through art, literature, scholarship, exhibitions, and field research. The Center's Cotton Mather Library in Arthur, Nebraska, its Martha A. Strawn Photographic Library in Davidson, North Carolina, and a ten-acre reserve along the Santa Fe River in Florida are available as retreats upon request.

The Center strives every day to make a difference through books, research, and education. For more information, please send inquiries to P.O. Box 23225, Santa Fe, NM 87502, U.S.A., or visit the Center's Website (www.americanplaces.org).

ABOUT THE BOOK:

The text for *The Last Harvest: Truck Farmers in the Deep South* was set in American Typewriter and Akzidenz Grotesk. The paper is acid-free Chinese Goldeast, 157 gsm weight. The book was printed and bound in China.

FOR THE CENTER FOR AMERICAN PLACES:

George F. Thompson, President and Publisher

Amber K. Lautigar, Publishing Liaison and Associate Editor

Ashleigh A. Frank and Laura E. Searfoss, Assistant Editors

Kristine K. Harmon, Manuscript Editor

David Skolkin, Book Designer and Art Director

Dave Keck, of Global Ink, Inc., Production Coordinator

PUBLISHER'S NOTES: *The Last Harvest: Truck Farmers in the Deep South* is the ninth volume in the series *Center Books on the American South*, George F. Thompson, series founder and director. The book was brought to publication in an edition of 1,500 hardcover copies, with the generous support of the Blue Earth Alliance and Friends of the Center for American Places, for which the publisher is most grateful. The publication of *The Last Harvest* coincides with a solo exhibition of Mr. Dilbeck's photographs at Callanwolde Gallery, in the Callanwolde Fine Arts Center, Atlanta, Georgia, September 15–October 27, 2006. A version of that exhibit can also be seen online: www.american-places.org. For more information about the Center for American Places and the publication of *The Last Harvest*, please see pages 98–99.

© 2006 Center for American Places
Photographs © 2006 Perry Dilbeck
Conclusion © 2006 Tom Rankin
All rights reserved.
Published 2006. First edition.
Printed in China on acid-free paper.

The Center for American Places, Inc.
P.O. Box 23225
Santa Fe, New Mexico 87502, U.S.A.
www.americanplaces.org

Distributed by the University of Georgia Press
www.ugapress.uga.edu

15 14 13 12 11 10 09 08 07 06   1 2 3 4 5

Library of Congress Cataloging-in-Publication Data is available from the publisher upon request.

ISBN 1-930066-49-X

Frontispiece: Pie Pans and Garden, Banks County, Georgia, 1998.
Photographs on pages iii and 1: America, 2003 and Jack Parris's Market, 2001.